THE SALVIFIC PLAN OF GOD FOR MANKIND

"Look, the Lamb of God, who takes away the sin of the world!" (John 1:29)

REV J.C. BANDA

'The Salvific Plan of God for Mankind' copyright © 2023
Rev. Josephat Chaponda Banda

The author has asserted his right to be identified as the author of this work in accordance with the Copyright, Designs and Patents Act 1988.

All rights reserved. No part of this publication may be reproduced, stored in a retrieval system, or transmitted, in any form or by any means, electronic, mechanical, photocopying, recording or otherwise without the prior permission of the author.

All Scripture quotations are taken from the New International Version, NIV Study Bible.

ISBN: 978-1-3999-5238-5

Table of Contents

Explanation of Greek Letters and Theological Symbols........4

Dedication..6

Acknowledgements..7

Introduction..8

CHAPTER 1
God and His People..11

CHAPTER 2
God and the Church...16

CHAPTER 3
Chapter 1..30

CHAPTER 4
Chapter 1..37

Explanation of Greek Letters and Theological Symbols

(A) ALPHA (The first letter of the Greek Alphabet)

(Ω) OMEGA (The last letter of the Greek alphabet)

(ALPHA and OMEGA)

JESUS CHRIST - The first and the last.

REVELATIONS 22:13

Jesus Christ is symbolically referred to as the unblemished sacrificial Lamb of God in God's salvific plan, to redeem mankind from sins and eternal death. Faith in God through Jesus, people are saved by God's grace. John 3:16

JOHN 1:29 (Agnus Dei [Latin] meaning Lamb of God.)

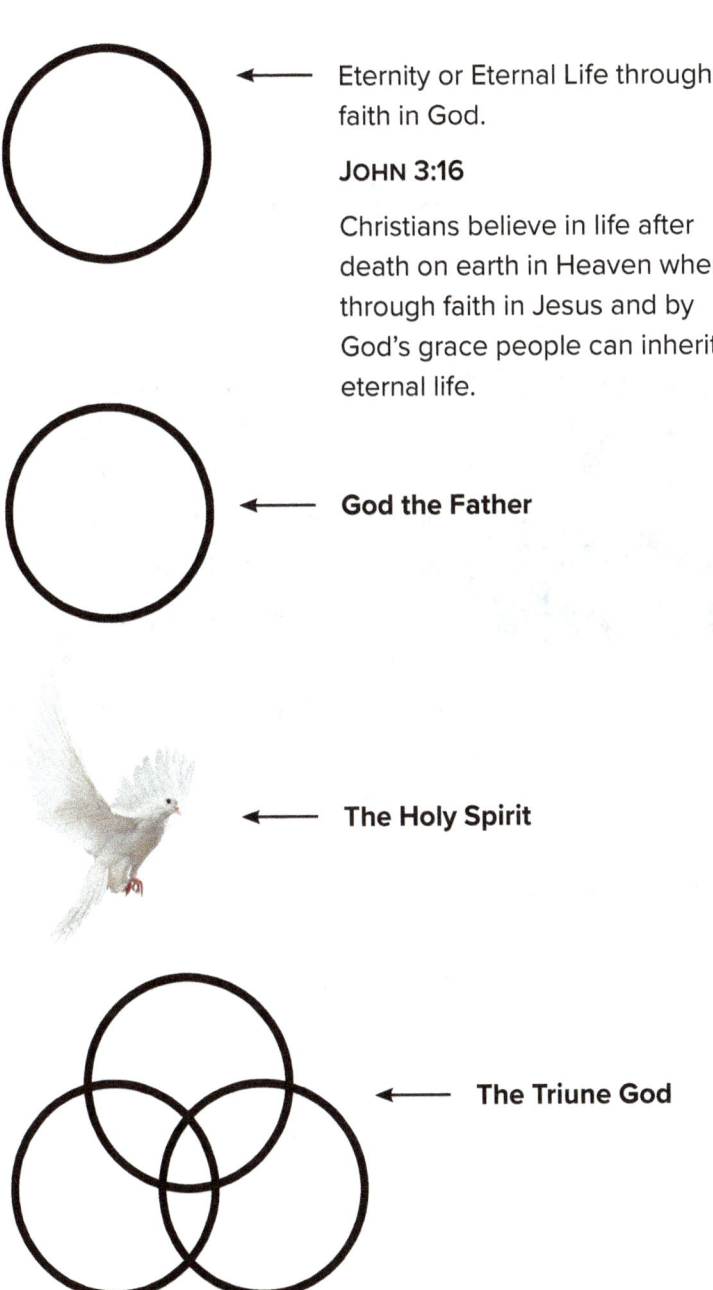

← Eternity or Eternal Life through faith in God.

JOHN 3:16

Christians believe in life after death on earth in Heaven where through faith in Jesus and by God's grace people can inherit eternal life.

← **God the Father**

← **The Holy Spirit**

← **The Triune God**

Dedication

This booklet is gratefully dedicated to my dear, prayerful wife, Mrs Mavis Nyandowe Banda, who is an inspiration to me. When she hears me speak something of theological interest, she quickly interjects a few positive words, encouraging me to put together my ideas into readable collections for the young and adults. These can then become food for thought for fellow sojourners in this world, as we journey tirelessly towards our permanent home, where we will join the Church triumphant. Any interested readers might find something in this booklet to enlighten them, and to bring them joy and liberation in the different aspects of life, through faith in the Triune God.

Rev Josephat Chaponda Banda

Acknowledgements

I am grateful to have received assistance from family members in the writing of this booklet. Typing and organisation of the work was undertaken by my son, Mr Shadreck Banda, and daughter, Mrs Thokozani Chiwara. Some editing was carried out by my son, Mr Habakkuk Banda, and by a volunteer interested in seeing the booklet published. My wife, Mrs Mavis Nyandowe Banda, also contributed through sharing her ideas to be included in the writing of the booklet.

Introduction

Generally, people have some concept of God. This is evidenced by the different names they give Him because of who He is and what He does in the world. When people miss the target of worshipping God, they resort to idolatry. **JAMES 2:19** says, "You believe that there is one God. Good! Even the demons believe that – and shudder." In the general revelation of God to mankind, through the created things and human conscience, people have come to know Him. Even the atheists who say there is no God have an idea that there is a God about whom they have heard from the theists. Things that don't exist have no names, hence they are unknown. Things that do exist have names people have given to them.

Because of human lack of understanding of God, there is a need to teach about God, for we were created by Him, for Him. He decided to make persons in His image who have a creative mind (homo sapiens), unlike other animals. Knowing God is to be wise, as is stated in the Bible (**PROVERBS 1:7**), because, as our Sovereign Ruler, we should know what He wants us to do, why we were created and where we are heading. People have a brighter future in eternity with their Creator if they obey Him and have faith in Him. For Christians, eternity with God is reached through faith in Jesus Christ,

INTRODUCTION

His only begotten Son and the perfect revelation of God the Father to mankind (**JOHN 3:16; 14:6–10**).

God loves all people although He hates the bad things they do, for He is holy. He guides His people in righteousness and protects them. He provides His people with air, water, food, light, soil, minerals and vegetation for their existence and welfare. Truly, there is no one like Him. God is invisible, immortal, omniscient, omnipresent and omnipotent. Because of what He is, mankind ought to worship Him in the Spirit and in truth for their salvation from sin and eternal death.

God has a salvation plan for mankind through Jesus, His Son, since we all fall short of His glory. He is involved in the salvation history of mankind, from birth to death. The destinies of people are shaped by what they do. Upright attitudes and deeds, through faith in Jesus, lead to eternal life, whereas evil attitudes and behaviour lead to eternal death, according to the salvific plan of God for mankind. In **JOHN 3:19–21**, John writes about God's verdict on human beings at the end of known time, on Judgement Day:

This is the verdict: light has come into the world, but people loved darkness instead of light because their deeds were evil. Everyone who does evil hates the light, and will not come into the light for fear that their deeds will be exposed. But whoever lives by the truth comes into the light, so that it may be seen plainly that what they have done has been done in the sight of God.

GOD'S SALVIFIC PLAN FOR MANKIND

The salvific plan of God for mankind is canonised in the Holy Bible for people to read and understand for their salvation. God's plan starts at the fall of Adam and Eve, or the first human beings, and its climax is in the death and resurrection of Jesus Christ, the Lamb of God, who died as an expiation for our sins (**JOHN 3:16**).

CHAPTER 1

God and His People

According to the Holy Bible, the Old Testament faith is fulfilled in the New Testament for the salvation of mankind. God's creation of the universe pleased God Himself: "God saw all that He had made, and it was very good. And there was evening, and there was morning – the sixth day" (**GENESIS 1:31**). There was no tempter and no sin, which, as time went on, are what made Adam and Eve fall spiritually, when they were misled to disobey God by the devil (**GENESIS 3:1–24**). Although the first human beings sinned against God, the gracious God who created them in His image still loved them – but hated their sin of disobedience. However, He deprived these first human beings of the benefits of living in the garden of Eden and of eternal life because of their sin, which resulted in a natural phenomenon of death that affected the prosperity of these first human beings forever.

The gracious God then put in place the means of saving mankind from sin (His salvific plan) so that He could remain the God of the people eternally. Obedience to what God says, or faith in Him, leads people to become God's chosen few to be saved eternally. Since people were created in the image of God, they were meant to do His will to maintain their righteous relationship with their Maker and the Ruler of the universe. The salvific plan of God for mankind, according to Christians, is canonised in the Holy Bible. Everything human beings need to know about what they should do to please God and to be saved from sin and eternal death has been revealed by Him in this precious Book. From the Holy Bible, theologians have come up with doctrines that seek to articulate the Christian faith in a coherent manner, so that heresies can easily be detected and exposed when they are taught deliberately or unknowingly in the Church.

In any Christian denomination, the fundamental doctrine to be taught is about the living God, known as the Triune God. He is God the Father, God the Son and God the Holy Spirit (**GENESIS 1:1–3; JOHN 1:1–4**). God the Father, God the Son and God the Holy Spirit are co-eternal. The doctrine of God is centred on God Himself, who took the initiative to reveal Himself in many ways to mankind. Through people's positive response to God's revelation, they acknowledge His existence and presence among them as one who brought things into being, and who should be obeyed and worshipped. His will is to be done by all the people created in His image in order to please Him, as expressed in **EXODUS 20:1–17** and **JOHN 3:16**.

God came to be known by people as the Creator of the universe and of the people themselves. They also acknowledged God as: omnipresent, omniscient, omnipotent, transcendent and gracious; keeper of orphans; lover of people; everlasting or immortal and invisible; holy; the Sovereign Ruler of the universe and the righteous Judge, who will justify the righteous people and condemn the sinful ones in His justice and holiness. Those who repent wholeheartedly, He forgives, but the impenitent, He condemns eternally (**ROMANS 1:18–32; 2:1–16**).

The Decalogue (Ten Commandments) and Faith in Jesus

For Christians, the Ten Commandments, which represent the will of God for mankind, are for guidance in spirituality and morality, but faith in God is through Jesus: "Agnus Dei" – the Lamb of God – brings about salvation from sin and eternal death (**JOHN 3:16**). Today, people cannot be saved by the law because of their inability to observe all the Ten Commandments every day of the year without violating at least one of them (**ROMANS 3:1–31; 7:1–25; 11:1–32; 13:1–14; MARK 10:18; JAMES 4:17**).

By believing in God through Jesus, who suffered and died as an expiation for people's sins, people can be saved from sin according to God's plan for our salvation. Jesus came to fulfil the law and, therefore, He supersedes the law. This means that what the Old Testament meant to achieve was achieved by Jesus Christ in the New Testament. Today, the blood of a sacrificial sheep or lamb cannot wash away our sins; only the blood of Jesus can do this (**HEBREWS 12:24; 1 JOHN 1:7**).

Christians affirm the cleansing of their sins by the blood of Jesus when they sing the hymn, "Nothing but the blood":

Nothing but the blood
Robert Lowry

What can wash away my sin?
Nothing but the blood of Jesus.
What can make me whole again?
Nothing but the blood of Jesus.

Chorus
O precious is the flow
That makes me white as snow;
No other fount I know;
Nothing but the blood of Jesus.

For my pardon this I see:
Nothing but the blood of Jesus.
For my cleansing this my plea:
Nothing but the blood of Jesus.

Nothing can for sin atone:
Nothing but the blood of Jesus.
Naught of good that I have done:
Nothing but the blood of Jesus.

This is all my hope and peace:
Nothing but the blood of Jesus.
This is all my righteousness:
Nothing but the blood of Jesus.

Faith without deeds is dead and good deeds without faith in God cannot make a person enter heaven. Faith coupled with good deeds can qualify one to enter heaven by God's grace (**JAMES 2:14-26; HOSEA 4: 1-19; AMOS 5:21-24**)

God's Prophets

The prophets were called and inspired by God to communicate His messages to the chosen people. These prophets delivered the messages to the people to turn them away from idolatry and other sinful behaviour. They were urged to keep their covenant with God and were warned against sinning, because sin incited the anger of God and it was punishable. The prophets of God advocated for the people's obedience to Him in order for them to maintain a right relationship with Him as the chosen people, with the responsibility to enlighten other nations about the true, living God, who was to be worshipped

CHAPTER 2

God and the Church

The Church, which is theologically known as the body of our Lord Jesus Christ, is made up of believers in God through Jesus Christ, called Christians. These Christian believers were called out of the world in order to serve God and the people in the world. The mission of the Church is to liberate people from sin and to establish righteousness and justice on earth in light of Jesus, who read from the book of Isaiah the text that referred to Himself:

The Spirit of the Lord is on me, because he has anointed me to proclaim good news to the poor. He has sent me to proclaim freedom for the prisoners and recovery of sight for the blind, to set the oppressed free, to proclaim the year of the Lord's favour.

LUKE 4:18–19

The gospel is the good news about Jesus, who came to liberate people from spiritual, mental and physical bondage. Since Christians form the body of Jesus, the mission of Jesus in the world is the mission of the Church.

God and the Church

Jesus Christ, the greatest teacher who has ever lived on earth, and the perfect revelation of God the Father, taught about the will of God. He also did things in agreement with God the Father. He taught His disciples the significance of obeying God; of love, sacrifice, holiness, repentance, endurance and mercifulness. After teaching the disciples, who became the apostles, Jesus sent them into the world to preach, teach and make disciples for Him (**MATTHEW 28:19–20**). The followers of Jesus should uphold His teachings for their spirituality and morality, in order to consolidate their upright relationship with God as they worship Him, and give their services in humility and love to mankind. When people are converted to Christianity, they become co-workers with Jesus in the world, where believers become obedient citizens of God's Kingdom. Through prevenient grace, justifying grace and sanctifying grace, believers are led to eternal life in heaven.

In His teachings, Jesus laid emphasis on loving God, as stated in **DEUTERONOMY 6:4–7**, as the first commandment to be observed by people. The second commandment, He says, is to love your neighbour as you love yourself (**MATTHEW 22:37–40; LUKE 10:27**). The Ten Commandments in the book of **EXODUS (20:1–17)** were summarised into two commandments by Jesus: a vertical relationship with God and a horizontal relationship with fellow people on earth. These two relationships suffice in the Christian worship of God. But any violation of one of these two relationships jeopardises people's righteous relationship with Him, and calls for remorse and repentance to allow His forgiveness. Christian believers should be engaged in self-introspection as they strive to live a clean life and to be in line with the will of God, for the transformation of the mind and of the society where they live.

Those who adopt the teachings of Jesus should try their best to experience the concept of realised eschatology, whereby they taste the heavenly life here on earth where there are so many temptations to overcome. James, the brother of our Lord Jesus, urges Christians to be spiritually strong and morally right: "Submit yourselves, then, to God. Resist the devil, and he will flee from you. Come near to God and he will come near to you. Wash your hands, you sinners, and purify your hearts, you double-minded" (**JAMES 4:7–8**).

To hunger and thirst after righteousness (**MATTHEW 5:6**) is a good instruction for one who aspires to establish a righteous relationship with God. It is God who provides people with spiritual food – the satisfying and inspiring word that is full of wisdom on doing good before God and people. Doing the will of God is what people ought to do to please Him and to be His obedient servants, who bear the fruit of the Spirit mentioned by Paul in his letter to the **GALATIANS (5:22– 25)**. Although perfection is not within the range of human possibility, we have to try our best to live a righteous or clean life. The ultimate goal of our satisfaction in perfection as Christians is in Jesus alone, the sinless one, since we cannot be perfect on our own.

Because of our sinfulness, we cannot be one hundred per cent perfect, no matter how much we may try on our own. Hence Christians are supposed to be dependent on Jesus, the most righteous or sinless one, through faith (**JOHN 3:16; ROMANS 3:25–26; 8:1–4**).

Reading the Holy Bible with understanding revives the soul to the extent of worshipping the living God, and sharing with others the spiritual wealth in it, through teaching the word and preaching it for their salvation from sin. As the word of God in the Holy Bible is read from time to time, the reader's understanding is deepened and the need to share it with others becomes compelling. This is what happened with Katherine Hankey, an English evangelist, who wrote a poem in London in 1866 while recovering from a serious illness. In 1867, this religious poem was put to music by William Howard Doane. Today, "Tell Me the Old, Old Story" has become a church hymn that urges those who hunger and thirst after righteousness to sing it from time to time:

Tell Me the Old, Old Story

Tell me the old, old story,
Of unseen things above,
Of Jesus and His glory,
Of Jesus and His love;
Tell me the story simply,
As to a little child,
For I am weak and weary,
And helpless and defiled.

Chorus
Tell me the old, old story,
Tell me the old, old story,
Tell me the old, old story,
Of Jesus and His love.

GOD'S SALVIFIC PLAN FOR MANKIND

Tell me the story slowly,
That I may take it in –
That wonderful redemption,
God's remedy for sin;
Tell me the story often,
For I forget so soon,
The "early dew" of morning
Has passed away at noon.

Tell me the story softly,
With earnest tones and grave;
Remember I'm the sinner
Whom Jesus came to save;
Tell me the story always,
If you would really be,
In any time of trouble,
A comforter to me.

Tell me the same old story,
When you have cause to fear
That this world's empty glory
Is costing me too dear;
And when the Lord's bright glory
Is dawning on my soul,
Tell me the old, old story:
"Christ Jesus makes thee whole."

God, the Provider and Greatest Carer of mankind

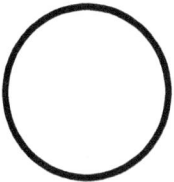

Love is the living God's attribute, hence in **1 JOHN 4:8** it is said that God is love. Because of what He is, He provides for people's needs and cares for them from birth to death. At the end of the known time on earth, He will raise them from the dead to allow them — His own people whom He has justified — to enter heaven to be with Him eternally.

By God's grace, all good things were given to mankind for their welfare. Misuse of them leads to the suffering of people. Some of the things given to human beings are easily accessible, whereas others are difficult to access for they are out of sight and buried underground, like the minerals. The wisdom found in the Holy Bible, the word of God, is like hidden treasure that has been excavated by people because of its significance. It is good for life on earth; it shows the way to eternal life in heaven, as testified by Jesus' apostles in the Gospels, their letters and the apocalyptic book of Revelation. The God-inspired writers of God wrote the books of the Bible to guide people spiritually and morally in order for them to live in good relationship with their Creator. In his second letter to Timothy, Paul makes it clear what the Bible is and why it was written: "All Scripture is God-breathed and is useful for teaching, rebuking, correcting and training in righteousness, so that the servant of God may be thoroughly equipped for every good work" (**2 Timothy 3:16–17**). In the Bible is the wisdom that is suitable for nurturing children to become people of integrity. Lack of such valuable knowledge can easily lead to spiritual weakness, or indecisiveness in dealing with social issues with clear conscience.

In our time, sceptical adults and naïve children seem to be increasingly anti-social because of a lack of fundamental moral standards to guide them. Every day, we make big or small decisions that make us do what's good or what's bad; right or wrong things to our own disgrace and remorse when they are against social norms or values.

To be faithful and dependable, people should be morally inclined towards what is good and right in light of the acceptable social principles that can distinguish human beings from animals in attitudes and behaviour. The writer strongly feels that the Bible, which some people avoid reading and trying to understand, has answers to many social problems that bring about strife in life. People were not born to suffer but to live well on earth, upholding theocentric principles of living while utilising the wealth given to them by God, like the soil, air, water, animals, vegetation and minerals. If this God-given wealth was shared fairly, with a fear of God, poverty, famine and even some ailments could easily be eliminated on earth.

People are expected to be diligent in order to earn a living by the sweat of their brow. Indolence, debauchery, poor attitudes to work, and stealing are behaviours that can be nipped in the bud as children grow to adulthood. In adults, such behaviours can be dealt with by consciously taking the opposite way, or working against evil feelings, as responsible citizens in society. The results of misleading practices should be weighed thoughtfully and abandoned, as they produce many more disadvantages than advantages, irrespective of their enticement. This is the sentiment expressed in the biblical decalogue (**EXODUS 20:1–17**). Faith in God is like a coin with two sides that give it its identity. On one side of faith is believing in God and on the other side is ethics – that is, practices congruent with the beliefs to be in line with God's will. In His sermon on the mount, Jesus emphasised the importance of putting into practice what He taught. Those who hear the teachings and put them into action are likened to a wise builder, while those who do not apply what they are taught are likened to a foolish builder (**MATTHEW 7:24–27**).

Effects of Disobedience in Society

Because of selfishness, people can be inclined more easily to vice than virtue. As a result, poverty, murder, wars and devaluation of human life will be the way of things on earth; love and misuse of money too. Money will be put to the best use in order to preserve power; to buy expensive weapons of war, which will be procured for protection and for the invasion of powerful or weaker nations for exploitative subjugation. If people opted to live in peace in the world, the money spent on building up weapons of war could be directed towards the uplifting of life standards for people, and towards development and prosperity in the world. God is the owner of the whole world whereas people are only stewards of God's creation. The good stewards are expected to look after what has been entrusted to them by God very carefully and to His satisfaction in order to be rewarded.

Adjustments in attitudes and behaviour so as to be in line with God's will, will change social situations for the better. Short life spans can be lengthened by adopting theocentric right attitudes to God and our fellow people. With these right attitudes, the natural, God-given principle of co-existence can be easily and joyfully adopted for the common good. Different people and governments, which have manifested some weaknesses in human relationships, can be transformed for the better. In some cases, people's ideologies have yielded suffering because of their exploitative nature. We need to be rational and innovative in order to discover what we can't see to have a better life. Amendments to ideologies are possible to achieve a better goal that will please large numbers of people. If biblical theocentric principles have not been tried so that people can enjoy a better life, why can we not have a taste of them? **PSALM 34:8–9** offers words that encourage us to taste what we have not yet tasted and compare past and new experiences: "Taste and see that the LORD is good; blessed is the one who takes refuge in him. Fear the LORD, you his holy people, for those who fear him lack nothing."

Be a Humble Follower of Jesus

The Bible tells the truth. Anything that is untrue has a source other than God, whose Son said, "I am the way and the truth and life. No one comes to the Father except through me" (**JOHN 14:6**). Those who are guided by the Lord will never stray. Pleasing God is our natural law when it comes to leading a righteous life. Any wrong that we do calls for remorse and

God and the Church

repentance so that we can be forgiven by God, as He does not compromise with sin.

Those who want to follow Jesus should deny themselves – that is, be humble and abandon their own will to follow that of God. There are times when our will goes against God's and when that's the case, we should discard ours to pursue His. In **MATTHEW 16:24–26**, Jesus says:

Whoever wants to be my disciple must deny themselves and take up their cross and follow me. For whoever wants to save their life will lose it, but whoever loses their life for me will find it. What good will it be for someone to gain the whole world, yet forfeit their soul? Or what can anyone give in exchange for their soul?

Sacrificial following of Jesus is unavoidable and beneficial to the doers, for they do not labour in vain for the Lord. Paul, in his letter to the **PHILIPPIANS 2:8**, said this about Jesus: "And being found in appearance as a man, he humbled himself by becoming obedient to death – even death on a cross!" Words of wisdom found in **PROVERBS 16:1–33** show us that God is in control of our destinies. The destiny of the wicked is destruction. The Lord hates the attitude of everyone who is arrogant and He will never let them escape punishment. Be loyal and faithful and God will forgive your sin. Obey God the Lord and nothing evil will happen to you. In **PROVERBS 16:7**, we are advised: "When the LORD takes pleasure in anyone's way, he causes their enemies to make peace with them."

Suffering for the Lord and for people by being obedient to the Lord, and serving people faithfully by preaching and teaching the word of God for their salvation, is of necessity. The book of Revelation urges Christians to do their work as followers of Jesus by clinging to their faith. Owing to the prevailing persecution of believers during the reign of Emperor Domitian in the Roman Empire, some Christians fell into apostasy. Those who continued to serve the Lord and the people during that time of persecution were told by John, the author of the book of Revelation, of visions of those who kept their faith until their death, victors dressed in white clothes in heaven (**REVELATION 7:9–17**).

Prayerfully, Christians should go into the world to serve God and people, according to Jesus' Great Commission found in **MATTHEW 28:19–20**:

> *Therefore go and make disciples of all nations, baptising them in the name of the Father and of the Son and of the Holy Spirit, and teaching them to obey everything I have commanded you. And surely I am with you always, to the very end of the age.*

The Church as an institution of salvation for mankind is a symbol of God's love to the people on earth. Salvation of people from sin and eternal death is by faith in Jesus and by God's grace.

God and the Church

A hymn of encouragement in carrying out Christian responsibilities in the Lord's vineyard, among many others, is "Guide Me, O Thou Great Jehovah". These words can be read and reflected upon or sung:

Guide Me O Thou Great Jehovah
William Williams (translated by Peter Williams)

Guide me, O thou great Jehovah,
Pilgrim through this barren land;
I am weak, but you are mighty;
Hold me with your powerful hand.
Bread of heaven, bread of heaven,
Feed me now and evermore,
Feed me now and evermore.

Open now the crystal fountain,
Where the healing waters flow.
Let the fire and cloudy pillar
Lead me all my journey through.
Strong Deliverer, strong Deliverer,
Ever be my strength and shield,
Ever be my strength and shield.

When I tread the verge of Jordan,
Bid my anxious fears subside.
Death of death, and hell's Destruction,
Land me safe on Canaan's side.
Songs of praises, songs of praises
I will ever sing to you,
I will ever sing to you.

God Is Ever Active in Human Lives to Guide and Protect Them

Since the creation of the universe, God has proved His attribute of love to mankind through His amazing grace of making a person both in His image – "Imago Dei" – and a steward of the created things. He endowed this person with a creative mind that is able to rationally know good and evil through their conscience, which is part of God's general revelation. The living God is at the beginning and end of human history on earth, to guide, advise, inspire, care for and protect His people. He loves all people but hates their sinful acts as He is holy. When the first ancestors of mankind – Adam and Eve – sinned against God by disobeying Him, He looked for them, with agape love, in their lost status; He cared for them for procreation as He'd promised them, but deprived them of their former benefits of everlasting life and abundant food given freely in the garden of Eden (**GENESIS 3:1–24**). By the sweat of their brow, they were to have their food now.

Owing to the inherent sin of Adam in human beings, called "original sin", people need God's help to overcome sinful tendencies that lead them to the devil's snares. Human beings are individually and collectively inclined towards virtue and vice. They need self-control to overcome temptations and sins. The supernatural God helps people to be strong spiritually, but they are misled by the devil to continue to sin or to become rebellious against God to please themselves. In **GALATIANS 5:16–17**, Paul writes:

> *So I say, live by the Spirit, and you will not gratify the desires of the flesh. For the flesh desires what is contrary to the Spirit, and the Spirit what is contrary to the flesh. They are in conflict with each other, so that you are not to do whatever you want.*

Then, in **ROMANS 7:15–20**, Paul talks about the problem of the dual nature of a person, who needs the guidance of the Holy Spirit in order to do good.

Through our consciences, we can hear the divine voice that urges us to do good in life, whether we are believers or non-believers. However, doing the good or right thing when devoid of faith in God cannot save us from sin. Yet faith complemented by deeds is commendable. The choice we make in doing things can be justifiable or condemnable in light of God's will.

The omniscient and omnipresent God sees, hears and intervenes in human situations to save people now, and leads them to eternity when they die clinging to their faith in Him through Jesus Christ, their only hope for salvation (**JOHN 3:16**). From the book of Genesis to the time of Jesus in the New Testament, we read about God's salvific history of mankind. The Acts of the Apostles and the letters of the apostles that follow the Gospels are affirmations of this salvation history, through faith in Jesus and by God's grace.

CHAPTER 3

Beware of the Secularisation of the Sacred

Holy things and practices should be revered as appropriate means of communicating with the transcendent God. Treating them as ordinary makes them lose their significance or desacralises them. Jesus spoke against the desacralisation of the temple when He saw people buying and selling there, because it was meant to be a place where God was worshipped (**MATTHEW 21:12–13**). Worshippers should approach a place of worship with reverence by creating an atmosphere conducive to worshipping, through singing and praying. Solemn reading of the Holy Bible and proclamation of the word of God should be observed. Church doctrines should not be tampered with, to avoid the infiltration of baseless heresies, which can dilute the faith that is meant to lead worshippers to salvation. Faith needs to be guarded seriously against secularisation. Believers in God are expected to be reliable and they should strive to act with a clear conscience and without any sense of guilt. Violation of theological and ethical standards makes the perpetrator of the deed a captive spiritually. Living in sin is living in bondage, from which one can be liberated by Jesus. He is the liberator, who read those words about Himself from the book of the prophet Isaiah:

Beware of the Secularisation of the Sacred

> "The Spirit of the Lord is on me, because he has anointed me to proclaim good news to the poor. He has sent me to proclaim freedom for the prisoners and recovery of sight for the blind, to set the oppressed free, to proclaim the year of the Lord's favour."
>
> **LUKE 4:18–19**

This is the mission of Jesus on earth, which is also the mission of the Church. Theologically, the Church is the body of Jesus. Liberation of people from bondage should be aimed at by the Church in carrying out their mission in the world. Some Christian denominations have borne in mind the establishment of churches or sanctuaries to nurture people's souls in this world of temptations and diverse cultural and philosophical influences.

Churches help people to focus on God, the source of all wisdom and knowledge, for their spirituality and morality. For intellectual development, schools have been built, and for physical liberation solely, hospitals have been established. The Church uses the holistic method to serve the whole person, who is body, soul and mind. Faith and scientific healing are complementary, for both aim to liberate a patient from ailments. However, the writer is opposed to the idea of resorting exclusively to faith healing, because scientific medicines are made from medicinal plants created by God, and their purpose is to heal. Those who heal are instruments of God used to fight against ailments, although some of them may not believe in God.

Some Christian believers have lost their lives through objecting to going to hospital, believing in faith healing only. Rational faith in light of God can save people's lives, especially children who cannot make their own decisions when they are taken ill. At times, adults who belong to sects opt to go to hospitals to be treated, and yet they forbid their children to be treated to the point of them losing their lives. But there are occasions when categorical, imperative ethics can be relegated in favour of situation ethics, which allow certain things to be done because it is fitting to do them without violating the will of God. Jesus gives an example of situation ethics in the Bible: **MARK 2:23–28; LUKE 6:1–5**. Laws are imperative for discipline, but where what is fitting is more suitable than what is imperative, what is fitting can be done to save life, or if deemed more advantageous.

Mushrooming of Churches

It is good to sincerely worship God without ulterior motives of being idolised, of cheating, of abusing church funds for self-enrichment or of commercialisation of the Church. The Church should be self-sufficient in supporting the functions for its smooth running. It should not be found wanting in giving support to the needy, such as orphans, the poor, the hungry and the sick. Christians are their brothers' and sisters' keepers. The concept of charity should be rife in the Church to improve other people's standards of life in society.

This reminds the writer of the school motto of Chisipiti High School in Harare, Zimbabwe, which reads in Latin thus: "Fons Vitae Caritas" – meaning, "Charity is the source of life". Because God provides freely, we who depend on

Beware of the Secularisation of the Sacred

Him have life. As we are given things for our survival, we should remember to share what we have with those in need. To love our neighbour as we love ourselves is a biblical commandment or principle to be followed, both to please God and to help our fellow people in need. Anyone in need of my help is my neighbour, as is explained in the parable of the Good Samaritan, the Gospel of **LUKE 10:25–37**.

Worshipping God should be in the Spirit and in truth, as stated in **JOHN 4:23–24** by Jesus:

Yet a time is coming and has now come when the true worshippers will worship the Father in the Spirit and in truth, for they are the kind of worshippers the Father seeks. God is spirit, and his worshippers must worship in the Spirit and in truth.

God can be worshipped in any place, but what is important is to be true in the Spirit of God, without any deceit, conceit or traits of self-aggrandisement. People should see the Church as a sanctuary for their relief, security or protection from things that can harm or torment them spiritually, psychologically and physically. The Church as an institution of salvation should be inviting, friendly, welcoming and comforting. Leaders and worshippers should try their best to observe what Paul says in his letter to Timothy:

> *And the Lord's servant must not be quarrelsome but must be kind to everyone, able to teach, not resentful. Opponents must be gently instructed, in the hope that God will grant them repentance leading them to a knowledge of the truth, and that they will come to their senses and escape from the trap of the devil, who has taken them captive to do his will.*
>
> **2 Timothy 2:24–26**

Church schisms demoralise worshippers to the extent of destroying the Church's mission, to our detriment. Love, humility, patience and endurance, as Christian virtues, should be utilised to make insurmountable social problems surmountable.

It is believed that some start their own denominations, sects or cults because of theological differences, a search for leadership power, or a passion for self-enrichment through church funds. This can lead to avarice and idolisation of the leader and money by the consistent teaching and preaching of a prosperity gospel. Such feelings in the Church tend to dampen people's enthusiasm in worshipping God in the Spirit and in truth. Some might go to places of worship only to find themselves in an impoverishing predicament spiritually, morally and economically, as they are urged to adopt idiosyncratic beliefs of getting healed by grazing on grass and getting rich quickly by seeding money. Giving such teachings to worshippers means they become sheepishly misled in their faith through idol worship that has been

Beware of the Secularisation of the Sacred

stealthily introduced into the Church. The denominations or sects based on the truth of God that sets us free from sin need to fear God more than any other group in executing what is acceptable in His sight, as is written in **PROVERBS 1:7**: "The fear of the LORD is the beginning of knowledge, but fools despise wisdom and instruction."

Reasoning in light of God is one way of doing theology. Paul, in his first letter to Timothy, warned him to be vigilant:

> *The Spirit clearly says that in later times some will abandon the faith and follow deceiving spirits and things taught by demons. Such teachings come through hypocritical liars, whose consciences have been seared as with a hot iron.*
>
> **1 TIMOTHY 4:1–2**

The words in 1 John 4:1–6 also remind the Church to be vigilant in order to test the spirits that visit them – are they genuine and leading them to God, or leading them elsewhere to perish? Jesus has said: "Watch and pray so that you will not fall into temptation. The spirit is willing, but the flesh is weak" (**MARK 14:38**).

Religious groups not built on a firm theological foundation can be misleading. There were false prophets in the past recorded in the Old Testament part of the Bible. They were employed by their rulers to tell them about their lives and their futures. The false prophets told them lies for fear of victimisation, and concealed the truth that liberates from sin.

However, the hidden truth surfaced as time went on.

The false prophets and those who listen to them and do what they say will perish, for falsehood is not part of the Kingdom of God on earth and in heaven. False prophets are mentioned in **1 Kings 22:1–40; Nehemiah 6:10–13; Jeremiah 23:13; Jeremiah 27:9–10; Matthew 7:15–20; and 2 Peter 2:1–9**, to reference a few verses in the Bible. Some false prophets pretend to be faith healers and to be able to raise people from the dead, so as to draw others to themselves. Most of these religious activities are done in the guise of faith healing, enveloped in a clandestine search for popularity and money to enrich themselves. Christians should be aware of the fact that we are living in the end of times, just before Jesus' Parousia (**2 Timothy 3:2**). When planting churches, religious leaders should guard against the infiltration of misleading doctrines from people holding ulterior motives. The apostle Paul gives good examples of protecting the Christian faith in his two letters to the Church of Corinth. The new converts easily show their naivety in faith, as, like sheep, they follow those who pretend to know what they are doing while holding fast to their hidden agenda of spiritual destruction. Those who profess to be Christians should have Jesus as the model and be humble before God in order to transform the world into a better place to live in.

CHAPTER 4

Let the Past, Present and Future Be Steps Towards the Ultimate Salvation:

God the Father, the Creator of the Universe

The Triune God we worship was there at the beginning of the creation of the universe, which He caused to be in existence. He is with the people, and will be there at the end of known time on earth in order to be with His saved children in eternity. Thus he will remain God of the living people eternally.

God the Father was convincingly known in His mysterious nature as One who spoke His creative word, known as the incarnate Word, later known as Jesus (**JOHN 1:1–4; MATTHEW 1:22; LUKE 1:31–33**. The Holy Spirit was and is eternally in the nature of God known as the Spirit or Spirit of God (**GENESIS 1:2**) in the Old Testament, and also in the New Testament, where He is known too as the Holy Spirit. The three Persons in one God work in agreement (**GENESIS 1:10–26; 1:27**). An encounter with one Person of the Deity is an encounter with the three Persons. Jesus taught Philip, His disciple, by saying:

> "Don't you know me, Philip, even after I have been among you such a long time? Anyone who has seen me has seen the Father. How can you say, "Show us the Father?" Don't you believe that I am in the Father, and that the Father is in me? The words I say to you I do not speak on my own authority. Rather, it is the Father, living in me, who is doing his work. Believe me when I say that I am in the Father and the Father is in me; or at least believe on the evidence of the works themselves."
>
> **JOHN 14:9–11**; additional reading **JOHN 14:1–18**

Those who profess to be Christians should continue to learn from Jesus, who came from the Father. They should be constant in their faith in Him by doing the will of the Lord. Love of amassing wealth at the expense of loving Jesus and the Father leads to spiritual demise that results in sinful actions. A wise believer seeks to run away from sin and the anger of God to be on a safe side spiritually, mentally and physically. Let us learn from the good things of the past in salvation history to be able to continue to travel the life journey with courage and hope to win the victory in Jesus Christ.

Jesus as God the Son for mankind (Emmanuel)

What baffled some of the contemporaries of Jesus in the past, and some people at present, was His incarnation. The myopic minds of human beings could not, and still

God the Father, the Creator of the Universe

cannot, see beyond the physical aspect of Jesus to see His divinity. Some noticed His supernatural aspects through His teachings, authority and miracles, and believed that He is the Son of God through the inspiration of God the Father (JOHN 1:29–34; MATTHEW 16:16–17; MATTHEW 7:29: MARK 1:22; MARK 2:4–6; JOHN 11:41; 44). But though some people did not accept, or do not accept, that Jesus is the Son of God, that does not theologically nullify Jesus' Sonship of God. Things in the spiritual realm can only be understood by faith, which links a believer to God to establish a righteous relationship with Him.

Jesus having come into the world, He lived in the Spirit of God the Father to fulfil His Father's will in saving people from sin and eternal death through Him. When Jesus lived on earth, the world experienced the presence of God the Father and God the Holy Spirit as well. The universal love of God to mankind was manifested in His Son Jesus, who died for the sins of mankind so that they could be saved through faith in Him.

When Jesus resurrected from the dead, a great miracle like His incarnation made the Church dauntless in being His followers as Christians, whose name is taken from His salvation title (Kristos) Christ. Christians are an army of salvation in the world against the devil and sinfulness. Jesus, who ascended into heaven, took the spiritual form of God, who is Spirit, invisible, omniscient and omnipresent. In His Great Commission to His disciples, Jesus said, "And surely I am with you always, to the very end of the age" (MATTHEW 28:20). Jesus is with the Church He founded as an institution of salvation forever.

The Triune God in the Life of the Church

God the Holy Spirit came into the world visibly, like tongues of fire upon the disciples of Jesus in the upper room in Jerusalem (**ACTS 2:1–13**). The promise of Jesus to His disciples was fulfilled (**JOHN 14:15–18; ACTS 1:5; 1:8**). As people await Jesus' Parousia, the second and final time visibly, the Holy Spirit is in control of the Church in its services to God and the people on earth.

Although the Holy Spirit is invisible, His activities in the Church and the world can be experienced in convicting people of their sinfulness and helping them to repent and accept Jesus as their personal Saviour. The Holy Spirit empowers believers to work in the Church and the world, using the gifts given to them (**1 CORINTHIANS 12:1–11**). The Holy Spirit gives spiritual guidance to believers in their lives and in their worship, so that the truth of God can be proclaimed to people for their transformation and sanctification. The Holy Spirit comforts people during difficult times of loneliness and bereavement. He advises people wisely what to do and accept to please God. The Holy Spirit also helps Christians in their weakness and intercedes for them (**ROMANS 8:26–27**). The three Persons of the Deity harmoniously work for the welfare and salvation of mankind.

Strong Christian believers are enabled to work hard in the Lord's vineyard to produce the fruit of the Holy Spirit mentioned in Paul's letter to the **GALATIANS** (**5:22–26**). To be a strong person spiritually and morally is always the aim, with the help of the Holy Spirit, who dwells in us as Christian believers. Humility is a Christian virtue that can help believers listen attentively to what the Spirit says, for us to do the will of God.

God the Father, the Creator of the Universe

Throughout Church history, devoted believers in God through faith in Jesus endured persecutions, because they were filled with the Holy Spirit. In the book of Acts, Peter said:

> "Rulers and elders of the people! If we are being called to account today for an act of kindness shown to a man who was lame and are being asked how he was healed, then know this, you and all the people of Israel: it is by the name of Jesus Christ of Nazareth, whom you crucified but whom God raised from the dead, that this man stands before you healed. Jesus is 'the stone you builders rejected, which has become the cornerstone.' Salvation is found in no one else, for there is no other name under heaven given to mankind by which we must be saved."
>
> **ACTS 4:8–12**

The Holy Spirit enables believers to be courageous enough to serve God and people sacrificially. Jesus said to a crowd, 'What good is it for someone to gain the whole world, yet forfeit their soul? Or what can anyone give in exchange for their soul?' (**MARK 8:36–37**). Although the world is a very wealthy gift given to mankind, in light of God it is not the exclusive wealth we need. There is spiritual wealth, which is complementary to earthly wealth, and which leads to eternal life in heaven (**LUKE 12:13–21**).

The Church today, which is engaged in missiology for the evangelisation of the world, has a lot to learn from the book of Acts. This book is about the acts of the apostles of Jesus, but can also be viewed as the "Acts of the Holy Spirit". Later on in Church history, Christians were persecuted, but they continued to proclaim the word of God through the inspiration of the Holy Spirit.

They sang about the oneness of Christian believers, whose Lordship and foundation is Jesus Christ; they sang the hymn, "The Church's One Foundation" as they persevered to serve God and the people in the world. The hymn affirms the oneness of the denominations, although believers may uphold some doctrines that perhaps differ here and there. Because they all profess Jesus as their Lord and Saviour and were baptised in the name of the Triune God, they are God's children by adoption and coheirs with Jesus Christ. The hymn on the oneness of the Church in Jesus Christ, whose body it is, symbolises the oneness of Jesus with God the Father and God the Holy Spirit:

The Church's One Foundation
The Rev Samuel John Stone

The Church's one foundation
Is Jesus Christ, her Lord;
She is his new creation
By water and the Word:
From heav'n he came and sought her
To be his holy Bride;
With his own blood he bought her,
And for her life he died.

God the Father, the Creator of the Universe

Elect from every nation,
Yet one o'er all the earth,
Her charter of salvation,
One Lord, one faith, one birth;
One holy Name she blesses,
Partakes one holy food,
And to one hope she presses,
With every grace endued.

'Mid toil and tribulation,
And tumult of her war,
She waits the consummation
Of peace for evermore;
Till, with the vision glorious,
Her longing eyes are blest,
And the great Church victorious
Shall be the Church at rest.

Yet she on earth hath union
With God the Three in One,
And mystic sweet communion
With those whose rest is won:
O happy ones and holy!
Lord, give us grace that we,
Like them, the meek and lowly,
In love may dwell with thee.

The Church that is inspired by the Holy Spirit will always be restless in its search for the lost in order to show them the way to salvation. Since our life on earth is short, there is need to work diligently and expeditiously to make disciples for Jesus for their salvation. There is great joy in heaven for even one person who is born again in spirit. Jesus Christ said, "I tell you that in the same way there will be more rejoicing in heaven over one sinner who repents than over ninety-nine righteous people who do not need to repent" (**LUKE 15:7**).

The Church needs to be vigilant and stand firm as the apologists do in defending the Christian faith as a divine gift to the chosen ones. Those who follow God through Jesus have been graciously chosen by Him to be His children (**JOHN 15:16; ROMANS 8:28–30; EPHESIANS 1:4–5; 1:11–12**) and to be His faithful messengers in the world.

Paul's profound faith throws light on our calling by God in **1 CORINTHIANS 1:30–31**, where he says:

> *It is because of him that you are in Christ Jesus, who has become for us wisdom from God – that is, our righteousness, holiness and redemption. Therefore, as it is written: "Let the one who boasts boast in the Lord."*

The Holy Spirit enlightens the obscure verses of the Bible to help us understand them better. Though we are followers of Jesus and penitent sinners, we still fall short of God's glory (**ROMANS 3:23**). We need Jesus' assistance through faith in Jesus Himself, who is incorruptible or sinless, for our salvation from sin to qualify to enter heaven. Our perfection

God the Father, the Creator of the Universe

can be consummated in Jesus and Jesus alone, through faith and by God's grace (**JOHN 3:16**).

The Triune God has good plans for His people, provided they keep their covenant with Him, as was promised to the Jews under Babylonian captivity. God said to His people in captivity during the time of Jeremiah: "For I know the plans I have for you … plans to prosper you and not to harm you, plans to give you hope and a future" (**JEREMIAH 29:11**). When we cannot do what we are supposed to do according to the will of God, we are in captivity, as were the Jews alluded to in the text who were in political captivity. Our destinies are under God's control. However, disobedience has a negative end whereas positivity to God's will has a bright future, not only on earth but in the life to come. While we are on earth, suffering will be with us because this is where the devil can play his games; where he misleads people away from God's plan through personal desires and disobedience, or rebellious attitudes and behaviour against God's will. In **JAMES 1:13–15**, we are advised:

> *When tempted, no one should say, "God is tempting me." For God cannot be tempted by evil, nor does he tempt anyone; but each person is tempted when they are dragged away by their own evil desire and enticed. Then, after desire has conceived, it gives birth to sin; and sin, when it is full-grown, gives birth to death.*

Faith in God and self-control are strong weapons with which to fight against the devil's temptations.

GOD'S SALVIFIC PLAN FOR MANKIND

Although we are sinners, God has set a plan for us to be saved from sin through faith in Jesus Christ. We are made restless because of our personal and social sins, which cause us to perform below the mark spiritually and morally in the society. There is need for us to have regular self-examination spiritually and morally in order to discard bad practices that are unacceptable to God, although we may enjoy doing them. True joy is doing good things rather than doing bad ones. The source of doing evil is none other than the devil, who encourages us to do this against God our Maker and Owner, for whom we were created.

Fellow life-journey travellers, the unknown has been revealed by Jesus Christ, the true revelation of God the Father to mankind. Jesus said to Thomas, His disciple, as He continues to say to us today: "I am the way and the truth and the life. No one comes to the Father except through me" (**JOHN 14:6**). What Jesus says here affirms what John says: "For God so loved the world that he gave his one and only Son, that whoever believes in him shall not perish but have eternal life" (**JOHN 3:16**).

Let's cling to our faith in Jesus Christ against all odds for a crown of everlasting life in heaven. In the book of **REVELATION 21:4**, we read: "'He will wipe every tear from their eyes. There will be no more death' or mourning or crying or pain, for the old order of things has passed away." Paul, in his letter to the **ROMANS (8:18–19)** says: "I consider that our present sufferings are not worth comparing with the glory that will be revealed in us. For the creation waits in eager expectation for the children of God to be revealed."

There is a permanent home for the saved ones beyond the blue sky into which Jesus was seen ascending, in order to prepare for us a lovely dwelling place, full of eternal joy and peace in heaven.

Today, Christians nostalgically sing this hymn with hope:

In the Sweet By and By
Sanford Fillmore Bennett

There's a land that is fairer than day,
And by faith we can see it afar,
For the Father waits over the way
To prepare us a dwelling place there.

Refrain
In the sweet by and by,
We shall meet on that beautiful shore;
In the sweet by and by,
We shall meet on that beautiful shore.

We shall sing on that beautiful shore
The melodious songs of the blest;
And our spirits shall sorrow no more –
Not a sigh for the blessing of rest.

To our bountiful Father above
We will offer our tribute of praise
For the glorious gift of His love
And the blessings that hallow our days.

GOD'S SALVIFIC PLAN FOR MANKIND

What God promises, He fulfils to be immutable according to His nature. Let's prepare for the future life without neglecting our life here on earth. The heavenly banquet is to be tasted here on earth, hoping to have it consummated in heaven.

Living in abundance on earth is also part of Jesus' mission here. For Jesus Himself said, "The thief comes only to steal and kill and destroy; I have come that they may have life, and have it to the full" (**JOHN 10:10**). Let's care for the body, soul and mind for our welfare not only on earth but in heaven also, where there is no suffering, hunger, death and mourning eternally.

"Deus semper Invictus est." (Latin)

"God is always invincible." (English)

www.ingramcontent.com/pod-product-compliance
Lightning Source LLC
Chambersburg PA
CBHW050449010526